POEMS FROM THE PINNACLE

POEMS FROM THE PINNACLE

JOHN ELLIS

ISBN-13: 9781545057759
ISBN-10: 1545057753
Library of Congress Control Number: 2017905119
CreateSpace Independent Publishing Platform
North Charleston, South Carolina

DEDICATION

**With grateful
appreciation to the
wonderful Pinnacle
residents who are
friends to us, pray for
us, help us, encourage
us daily, and have now
become a loving family**

INTRODUCTION

—⋙—

These poems tell who I am, what I think, how I hope. After 80 years on this planet, I want to share with others some poetry I have written as my "birthday gift."

Poems are a genre intended to grab with intensity. Mine speak to daily events and challenges. Some, hopefully, reflect wisdom. A few are whimsical; others are nostalgic. All are intended to give insight into the complex through simplicity.

I pray that all who read and ponder these poems will ignite their interest in the human story, and, by their lives, will add to its beauty.

SENIOR LIVING

In modern parlance it is a "senior living residence"
A lifestyle designed for comfort and control
Coping with the vicissitudes of old age
A strategy for living in and exiting this world with dignity.

The concerns of children and spouses are soothed
Knowing that activities with care and concern abound
Life can be lived gratefully with exuberance and joy
Giving God thanks for the precious gift of each day.

Our resident companions become a loving extended family
We are fascinated by the life stories of new friends
We pray fervently for those who need medical attention
And sadly a few pass on to their eternal reward.

We learn that wisdom resides in those with plentiful experience
God has a remarkable way of informing his children in maturity
We seek to be compassionate, empathetic, and sharing
Knowing that each of us is created in the image of God.

Senior living can be cruel for some or an exciting journey
Minds can be stolen by Alzheimers, bodies racked by pain
The wise learn it is not only what happens but how we react
Ultimately God is in control. In our deepest being we can trust him.

SENIOR LEARNING

Lifetime learning is the current admonition
Keep learning and grow, whatever your condition
That's easy to say and much harder to do
To keep trying and learn something that's new.

Our memory can plague us and not be our friend
Unlike using our computer we can't just hit "send"
We sit and we wrestle with some message to retrieve
When it doesn't come quickly we still must believe.

Yes, "belief" is one secret we must hold onto for life
Trust in God, believe in ourselves, throughout all the strife
We can keep on learning and thus stimulate our minds
Aging is no picnic but new learning helps us shine.

We are given wonderful bodies even though they grow old
It helps to think positively and focus our minds on the bold
Yes keep on learning and trying, why not give it your all
Learn to be grateful and make your life a ball.

WE'RE FAMILY

Pinnacle living is a precious time of life
Maturity has a way of reducing options
At the Pinnacle our choices are multiplied
We are blessed by a new extended family.

Folks living here have survived tough times
They are talented and have served in many roles
It is delightful to hear their storied histories
Together we face each day with renewed gratitude.

"We're family," we say, and we care deeply about each other
In our mature state it is necessary to see the doctor
Hopefully, simply for maintenance but complications occur
We have learned to pray for one another: we're family.

We know that many of us are living in our latter days
We are grateful to God for life and for our daily breath
It is comforting to know that when we face life's tough challenges
We take care of one another: "We're family."

VIBRATIONS

In Beijing two bell towers loom on elevated land
Within one an ancient drum sleeps in crumpled leather
Sitting in silence as awed eyes look and imagine
Days when its pulsing throbs passed along to reach the wall.

Testing the outer limits then of a vibrant kingdom
A dynamic culture, remarkably creative, a secretive civilization
That stuns us now with art, inventions, even terra cotta warriors
And two thousand miles of a brick and stone masterpiece.

What manner of men stood here atop the Bell Tower
To beat the drum and send its vibrations to alert the city
Or heard the messages passed pounding drum by drum
In pulsing beats that slowly informed those within the wall.

The horsemen and foot-soldiers warily patrolling
Watchful eyes and ears they sought to protect
A seminal time and culture now long vanished
But remnants of a wall and the towers still stand.

How frequently has that drum been summoned to life
To send a message of alarm or routine reporting
Sometimes a celebratory roll, the cacophony of victory
Or the nervous throb of not knowing—uncertainty.

The centuries pass and remnants of the wall still stand
In the Capital the ancient drum sits in tattered mystery
Silenced now yet thousands come to gaze and marvel
The perseverance of stilled voices that built the undulating wonder.

A new civilization is now emerging as bursting from a cocoon
Displaying proudly a vast complexity few know or understand
Seeking its place in a modern multi-cultural interconnected world
Seething with nations new and old and conflicted by restless disso-
nance.

What messages now will the "Tower Land" send the world
No drum delay but instant receipt of vibrations in an internet age
Will the messages contain the hope of reconciliation and cooperation
Or will fear and belligerence dominate the modern drumming.

What if the wisdom embedded in the ancient drum could be unlocked
The crumpled leather unleashing its hidden secrets for human-kind
Throbbing metaphorically to challenge us to listen beyond any wall
Vibrating softly: Be grateful; Seek peace; Always love one another.

ACTIVITIES

—∿∿—

Life for seniors can be a time of winding down, withdrawal, or participating in a new venture. The Pinnacle lets you choose, but encourages building relationships with others and entering into the activities. The choices are many: trips; exercise; dining; learning; special programs; entertainment; and worship. The options offer something for everyone.

This section of poetry portrays the vibrancy of the Pinnacle family and many of its diverse activities.

CLUTTER

We all "downsized" in order to move in
Hopefully thinking this "sizing" would last
Confident that in our lovely new home
Clutter would be a thing in our past.

We soon found the closets were far too small
We had brought too much to really fit in
So we fitfully sorted with tears in our eyes
Parting with this garment seemed like a sin.

We finally managed to get things under control
The arguments ended with an occasional mutter
We settled down living our life with satisfaction
We had won a victory against that demon clutter.

The months went by and we started to notice
Trinkets and books and memorabilia sprout
Clothes grow and grow while still in the closet
Our old demon clutter has moved in not out.

We love living here with lots of new friends
There are activities aplenty and time to putter
We don't cook much and a maid comes to clean
But the battle has been lost to that old demon clutter

STRENGTH AND BALANCE

Seniors must faithfully exercise their bodies
All the fitness gurus stress the need
It sometimes hurts and may cause us strain
The road to good health traverses thru pain.

Jena helps build our strength and our balance
Through her demanding, encouraging requests
We fitfully comply with the twist and the bend
Trusting one of these days our body will mend.

"Grab the weights now," she exhorts, calmly
We select the ones that seem right for us
We thrust them upwards and extend them out
Oh, this is helping, we have no doubt.

There's a thirty second drill of balancing on one leg
Keeping our core strong, staring at a fixed point
We shift to the other leg hoping it might be strong
"Just keep trying," she exclaims, "you can't do this wrong."

We try to settle down as we run slowly in place
But Jena zings us: "Pick up the pace."
We do knee bends, jumping jacks, stick out our rumps
Jena prepares us to face life's many bumps.

Time finally expires as we are catching our breath
"Good job, please sit, and let's stretch it out"
We dutifully bend forward keeping our backs straight
Hands high we breath deeply, more oxygen is great.

THE DINING ROOM

The Pinnacle dining room is a remarkable place
There we form friendships and build new relationships
We eat, of course, and sometimes complain
A menu pleasing to all is tough to maintain.

Families used to gather around the kitchen table
Talking, they formed unique values and deep loyalties
Pundits opine that such scenes are missing today
Noses buried in cell phones is the new family play.

Seating at the Pinnacle restores old family customs
Many let time and chance select their tablemates
Creating a welcoming mien for all who dine
Building a sense of community that lasts over time.

We need each other we have learned through maturity
We could be tempted to stay in our rooms and withdraw
But dining brings us together to form an extended family
Hearing trials and tales we now can repeat from memory.

We grow fond of each other and respond with genuine caring
Praying in gratefulness for blessings and relief from the pains
We find our fellow residents are a source of our delight
Dining at the Pinnacle helps us get through the night.

The dining room creates a special place where we relate
Complaining, laughing, teasing, encouraging one another
It is good for our souls to spend our precious time together
We're fortified by friendships to face any kind of weather.

There are too few times in our modern culture
Where we sit down and see one another face to face
Our busy lives in retirement can rob us even of taste
Let's slow down and relax in our special dining place.

HOITI TOIT

The Pinnacle folks are a lively lot
They travel to places to play
They'll go to a bar like the Hoiti Toit
And hoist their drink of the day.

They'll travel off to Trader Joes
To purchase "three buck chuck"
They'll find bargains galore there
It doesn't take much luck.

They'll head on off to Canyon Dam
Where the trails can almost break
Up and down but they persist
Till their poor knees start to ache.

Perhaps it's a walk in Landa Park
Where they rise up early in the morn
They feed the deer, the ducks and squirrels
Releasing endorphins to help feel reborn.

If you want an activity not on the list
Just make your request to our Kaye
She'll see how many would like to go
Then you can head out for the day.

You can dance or play at the Pinnacle
You can travel or you can just sit
Just be who you are and be yourself
You'll find you will be a great fit.

CHAIR YOGA

Yoga sounds too strenuous for seniors
It's hard to get up and down from the floor
If the teacher would say "lie flat" and do contortions
We would stop trying and look for the door.

Adaptation is now part of our cultural melieu
Bonnie, our Yoga teacher, is a master at that
She lets us stand and also sit in our chairs
It's far better than being prone on our mat.

She reminds us that falling is a pitfall in aging
"Good balance," she proclaims, should be our aim
So we stand on one foot lightly holding the chair
Core tight, focusing, wobbling, our balance to regain.

We stand up like good soldiers doing warrior poses
Warrior 1, arms raised aloft, then we shift to Warrior 2
Chest high, back straight, hands steady like our breath
We stare intently over a fingertip, no enemy in view.

Deep breathing is essential if we want to keep living
So we have lots of practice in how to breathe well
We breathe in calmly and hold it for twenty counts
When we control letting it out slowly we really feel swell.

The time passes quickly as Bonnie encourages us
Try to practice on your own, even a little every day
You will feel better, be more flexible, your body will glow
She smiles, thanks us for coming, and bows: "namaste."

THE PUZZLERS

Some folks at the Pinnacle love picture puzzles
They state intently at pieces all gone astrew
They look for a pair or two or three that will fit
Hoping the connections will come into view.

Life is a lot like doing jigsaw puzzles
Things are discombobulated and out of whack
You have to keep trying to put things together
Selecting the right pieces to get life back on track.

The puzzlers sit and stare with great patience
It takes a keen eye and a subtle perception
Their goal is to recreate a beautiful picture
Sometimes frustration is their only reception.

You could be a puzzler too if you are willing to ponder
Persevering and testing, staring at the clutter
It's a test of one's will and your firm determination
Puzzlers tease out the beauty while they silently mutter.

Puzzlers are tenacious focusing like lasers on the task
They find pieces that fit and renew their motivation
They find completion in choosing wisely and then connecting
A gorgeous picture emerges for our pleasure and reflection.

LINE DANCING

Line dancing has become a lot of good fun
Folks line up to hear music and learn a new step
Marge pushes and prods; says please keep the beat
Hold your head high don't stare at your feet.

They delight us with performances to entertain
Pirouetting and high stepping they dance gracefully
They wear colorful costumes and stay all in sync
I've suggested a name; they say: "Go take a drink."

Their routines get more fancy and coordination quite smooth
They gently sway their arms and they wiggle their rears
Their dances are now done with a measure of grace
They have learned to truly liven up the place.

So this "No Name" group has achieved sophistication
They spin in unison and create a great sight
Our line dancers are skillful as they do their thing
We cheer them on and love the pleasure they bring.

CARD GAMES

Lots of Pinnacle people play cards
It's a source of fun and relaxation.
The Foothills Lounge is their favorite place
Tackling bridge, samba and card concoctions.

Card games have little appeal for me
I grew up in a conservative Baptist home
Where "cards" were the Devil's handmaids
That could subtly cause my heart to roam.

I look in the windows and see focused faces
Cards curled protectively against the chest
Sometimes laughter and smiling prevail
Sometimes intensity to see who is best.

I reflect on the wonder of God's many gifts
Mind challenging games and escape from the day
The camaraderie of being together to have fun
The appeal is great; someday I might play.

THE HELPERS

Some precious people are born with the helper gene
They find their life's work in helping the hurting
Signing on as a life assistant they become a friend
Visiting or staying daily with someone in need.

It's a demanding role since patient needs are diverse
For some, it's get the daily meals and walk the dog
Help with daily bath, pills, and other personal needs
They generously give of themselves to nurture others.

Friendships develop as long conversations ensue
Tales of lost spouses are shared and memories recounted
Symbiotically, the helper, senses the needs and provides
Lovingly caring for their patient with tender assistance.

Some patients falter and go to their heavenly reward
The helper mourns with the family and keeps providing
Their task now done they sense another personal loss
They move on to another: They have God's helper gene.

TROPHIES

Life is consumed with striving
We are attracted to many things
Wanting, wanting we pursue trophies
Seeking the pleasure they bring.

Some trophies represent victories won
We display them proudly on our shelf
Other trophies are more ephemeral
We seek them trying to please ourselves.

As time elapses and new challenges appear
We're caught in a race to win once again
Most things that we seek rarely satisfy
We learn that self seeking brings little gain.

In maturity the trophies we once so admired
Lose their luster; we don't value them anymore
We learn that gratitude, kindness, and compassion
Bring happiness and satisfaction far more.

MUSIC

Music is clearly a gift from God
To calm us, inspire us, and light our way
With comfort and richness come what may.

There are genres galore to please every soul
We can chose ancient or modern, fast or slow
Daylight or night time wherever we go.

When we are troubled music is always around
We can relax and be nurtured by the beat
Deep in our minds it brings healing heat.

Music goes with us when we exercise
It stimulates our muscles as we groan
We forget fatigue and stop our moan.

Music reminds us we are vibrating beings
Sensing the melodies of the universe in the air
Restoring our souls freeing us from despair.

HAPPY HOUR

It is a quaint custom to designate a time
When folks assemble to consume alcohol
Happiness ought to come from within
Not requiring elixir to help have a ball.

The Pinnacle people assemble on Friday
Carrying beer and wine and special treats
Smiling jovially we great one another
Celebrating our survival one more week.

We gather around tables and sip our drinks
Sharing our snacks and some tasty libations
Hearing about the latest illness or operation
It's a convivial time of mini-celebration.

Alas the time, and tales, and the drinks run out
We unsteadily rise and pace to the dining room
It's hard to eat again when we are now so full
But at Happy Hour we've said good-by to gloom.

I think our quaint custom has a lot to commend
Life has challenging times and lots of pain
We can lift our glasses and share our joys
Happy Hour is a practice we should maintain.

PETS

The Pinnacle residents love their pets
But their choices are quite restrained
Dogs must weigh twenty-five pounds or less
Cats just have to be maintained.

Dog owners keep taking them outside
Mornings, afternoon, and sometimes at night
Cat owners hide their Cheshire grin
Their cats are tidy and never bite.

The other types of pets may exist
But about them we never hear
Goldfish, snakes, gerbils, perhaps
These don't need licenses every year.

As folks grow old companionship matters
We can be crotchety, lonely, and be no fun
Our pets overlook such human shortcomings
They love us anyway and friends they become.

There are cleanups and feeding to do
And the unwelcome trips to the vets
But the love they show us every day
Makes us rejoice that we have pets.

THE POOL

The Pinnacle has a splendid pool
It's heated for those who cherish warmth
A sybaritic appeal to submerge our cares
Soothing water to refresh our spirits.

Programs exist to lure us to enter
Water aerobics to strengthen our limbs
Energetic instructors who spur us on
Floats to assist us and help us to play.

Why does a a pool have such an appeal?
Does it return us to the womb and its primal splash?
Do we faintly feel the ocean's relentless tug?
Perhaps it suggests cleansing inside and out.

Simply looking at the calm water brings pleasure
The Pinnacle pool structure is open to the sky
The waterfall flowing adds to the pool's ambiance
Don't just admire it, plunge in, join the dance.

LEARNING

To learn is to be; it's a birthright
Our first teachers are our parents
They teach us the basics and even more
Their attitudes and values form our floor.

School teachers stress lifetime learning
Advising sternly that we can't ever stop
No matter how far we progress in school
If we ever stop learning we are a fool.

"We learn by doing," John Dewey once said
That's true but we learn in many different ways
Books, lectures, experiences and now the internet
Lessons emerge everywhere that's a sure bet.

When we're older learning slows down
Things that came easily now produce stress
We know a mind is a terrible thing to waste
So we hang in there learning at a much slower pace

Learning is a treasure of both pleasure and pain
Lessons can inform, inspire or cause great remorse
In maturity we more fully grasp the meaning of life
We understand that real learning requires some strife.

When we're ready to exit this mortal frame
We may regret things we didn't learn to do
But a clearer perspective tells us to never forget
That God loves us; He is not finished with us yet.

VITALITY

It's the zing, the fizz of life
That can vanish in maturity
Losing a step is par on life's course
For the folks on social security.

Some folks remain zestful as they age
They refuse the curse of Father Time
They remain grateful whatever comes
There is no hill they can not climb.

Remaining vital in our mind and body
Requires our diligence every day
Diet, exercise, doing good for someone
Giving and sharing is the only way.

An illness can crush and sap our spirit
The loss of loved ones can pierce our heart
Remaining vital in times of discouragement
Means keep striving; trust in God: It's an art.

THE JOY OF READING

Joy is a state of mind hard to achieve
Life's challenges press in to steal joy away
A search for joy finds little success in the exotic
Simply reading can bring us joy every day.

There are endless possibilities of things to read
Our Bible, the newspaper, books, electronic wares
They take us places we can scarcely imagine
They excite us, inform, inspire and remove care.

Even those with lost sight can read through hearing
It is a joy available in early morn, noon or night
Watching young children break the code to reading
Smiles on their faces they show pure delight.

The joy of reading is a gift given from the past
We can read in our homes or wherever we deploy
It's a pleasure available to the rich and the poor
So check out some reading and experience this joy.

LAUGHTER

Laughter is one of God's lubricants
It is a gift designed to delight and heal
Life can be tedious, boring and cruel
Laughter relieves and gives life appeal.

Some sources of healing have a vast cost
Choosing laughter is really quite a deal
You can spend it without cash or a credit card
It's an emotional nutrition just like a good meal.

Choosing the morose path and doing a sulk
Rarely helps one to cope with what is wrong
But laughing releases endorphins to soothe us
It's emollients help us break out in a song.

There are times when laughter is a poor choice
When others hurt deeply or are suffering grief
Much of the time, though, we shortchange ourselves
When we neglect to use laughter we lose sweet relief.

Let's summon laughter, then, when times get tough
When we're lonely, or sad, or grouchy as sin
Laughter is our friend that lightens our way
Use precious laughter, let sunshine come in.

THE STAFF

The Pinnacle staff is a remarkable group
How recruited I will never know
Inevitably they show us kindness and care
Day in, day out, they serve and don't slow.

The Pinnacle DNA began far in the past
In a home for retired pastors now open to all
Church based was the start and continues today
God's essence began it and it will not stall.

From managers to workers they give their best
They try to be helpful bringing comfort and cheer
They go out of our way to meet all our requests
We can comfortably ask them without any fear.

We're grateful for the blessing the staff brings
They're a wonderful addition to our life
They smile though hard pressed and listen a lot
Their goal is to smooth things and remove our strife.

THE WORKSHOP

A cottage is devoted to a workshop with tools
There is a lathe, a jigsaw, sanders and drills
Mostly men go there now with unique diligence
They fashion their projects with unusual skill

They work mostly in wood but also in metal
Ken cuts his glass and remains in fine fettle
The products they make they sometimes display
They sell at the craft show held across the way.

God has given us hands to help smooth our path
We also hold them up to worship and pray
When we enjoy the gift of fashioning with our hands
It recaptures our youth and reminds us of play.

Mind games are good and reading as well
We're not one dimensional as anyone could say
Creating with our hands brings a special bliss
It refreshes our souls we forget we are clay.

THE BISTRO

We like to eat, something we all can still do
Our dining room fare is typically delicious
Sometimes we crave a variety in taste
We head for the Bistro; there's no time to waste.

It's a neat place and is staffed by our best
Offering soup, sandwiches and a daily special
They serve the food with their charming flare
It's an informal place to grab your grub there.

They will cook you an omelet, fry you an egg
Make a special sandwich if you really desire
They wear chef's hats but are not certified cooks
But you couldn't tell that by our satisfied looks.

We love our little Bistro and the joy that it brings
At breakfast or noon we can change up on things
The camaraderie of dining at a tiny table for three
May bother a few but it's just right for me.

Section 2

CHALLENGES

—⟶⟶⟶—

Maturity brings many challenges. Health can deteriorate, surgery can be required, spouses and friends can go on to their eternal reward, and life can become depressing. In times like these the Pinnacle family lovingly provides support and caring. Life is too difficult to manage alone. We all need help. Embedded in the DNA of the Pinnacle is Christ's love. It is reflected in the caring actions of the residents. Challenges are inevitable. We are here to help one another.

This section of poetry reflects the profound complexity of living in maturity and the trust and faith we need in one another and in our Creator.

LOSS

Loss is a profoundly dispiriting word
We don't like to lose our keys or a contest
Such loses are momentary disruptions
But some loses lead to deep despair.

A child, spouse, mother, father, friend
Loses like these impact our soul
Creating within us an icy space
A hole that freezes over and remains.

How can we cope with such a loss
It's a test that most will face someday
We must trust that God will provide comfort
When it seems the heavens have become brass.

Loss in life is one bane of existence
Tearing apart our very foundation
With faltering prayers we can importune
When in the future we see only gloom.

Family and friends must come around
Even though precious few remain
Offering comfort and prayers, being present
Resisting the impulse to invoke false cheer.

The icy hole that freezes our soul
Will dissipate with time if not fully disappear
The rising sun and nature's new displays
Confirm that God will lead us into a new day.

VICISSITUDES

Life can be cruel and heartless
Hitting us in unsuspecting ways
Causing us to moan and suffer
Lamenting what has come this day.

No one promises that life will be easy
That's especially true as we mature
We lose strength, health, even our spouses
We plaintively ask God why we should endure.

Even our memories tend to fail us
Our minds can be robbed by a dread disease
The aches and pains persist with intensity
Happiness now seems only a tease.

In our fog we intuitively remember
We are a child of God and He truly cares
This life is only a shadow of what is coming
His love welcomes us up those golden stairs.

RECUPERATION

Recuperation can be a slow slog
Fighting back against an illness
That has threateningly laid you low
Sapping your strength midst stress.

Our bodies are a great gift from God
In our human flesh we are vulnerable
Pneumonia, falls, colds, heart, operations
There is a force that pulls us downward.

We feel weak wondering if recovery exists
Discouragement and despair engulf us
Is this the time we see our Maker, we ponder
It is a low period and we think and suffer.

Our family and friends sustain us in prayer
We remember past times when we have healed
A faint sense of optimism begins to infuse us
We have hope that we can be whole once again.

Sometimes, in spite of faith and fervent prayer
Our span on earth has run and we are ultimately healed
Returning to our Heavenly Father for our reward
Thankfully, we can also hear: "Stay and show my love."

REGRETS

Who does not regret?
Feel remorse over a failure
Condemn oneself for a deed or spoken word
Which, once completed, can never be undone.

I've lived long now with many regrets
Digging deeply into my past I exhume them
Most, to my surprise, are deeds undone
Thoughts not expressed, paths not taken.

We live a life of complex uncertainty
Fear and doubt can block our best intentions
What advice can we now give to the young?
Fear not; rise above failure; forgive; become love.

PATIENCE

Our mother told us to be patient
It was hard to understand what that meant
We waited in line and started to cry
Our patience had all been spent.

Maturity challenges us to reach a new level
Mom's admonitions were valid and still apply
There are still lines to endure, traffic to face
We remember big boys and big girls don't cry.

Sitting in a doctor's office well beyond the time
Holding endlessly on the phone for a human voice
Waiting for a medical report or a package to arrive
It's clear that patience is not our first choice.

As we add years of trials and our bodies get weak
One would think that our patience would grow
Our egos are precious and we think we have rights
So we bluster resentfully and bring on more woe.

Will we ever learn to live without growing so tense
When we're forced to wait and things don't go our way
The world is complex and we must finally understand
Mom was right: count to ten; and remember to pray.

HEALTH

Good health is the condition we all desire
It's the "sine qua non" to living well
The young think it will last forever
Losing it can cause one to face earthly hell.

In maturity we succumb to many illnesses
Our bodies weaken and we become less bold
We diet, exercise and take all our medicines
But the unfortunate truth is we all grow old.

Yet in maturity some folks still flourish
Is it their disciplined regime or fortunate genes
They sail along gamely impervious to age
Their bodies purring like an expensive machine.

Most folks in maturity have to watch carefully
They hope for the best and keep pushing ahead
Others grow weary and are tired of the fighting
They slowly move about but wish they were dead.

Good heath is assuredly a precious gift from God
Those with it know they are one of the blessed
We pray, we hope and we wonder what's next
It's best to be grateful, keep going, don't stress.

THE DARK DAYS

There are dark valleys in life
When life chaffs at our very soul
Nothing feels good or seems right
We are poured out to emptiness.

Weariness fastens its deep claws in us
Breathing is labored, we just want to quit
Rest escapes us as we steep in our lament
Has God condemned us to suffer forever?

We read that even saints have suffered thus
Wandering in their dark night of despair
Pondering why and desperately questioning
How a loving God could cruelly abandon them.

We are not comforted by knowing others suffer
What have I done that deserves such consignment
Why should life be so enervating, harsh and unfair
Have I been sentenced to Sheol before my time?

Time, though sometimes crushing, can also heal
Serendipitously we see a smile, a sunset or a dawning
Hope stirs deep within reminding us of God's promise:
"I will never leave or forsake you," and we begin to renew.

MEMORIES

The world changes while images remain
Events etched in my mind defying time
People and places I have encountered
Treasures to retrieve that are only mine.

Some memories I wish I could forget
Words I spoke I cannot take back
Things I did I now know I shouldn't
Rise up within not giving me slack.

Many memories bring me renewed glee
Happy times playing at the sunny beach
An athletic achievement and an award
That in maturity are now out of reach.

Our bodies grow feeble and start to fail
We cannot muster that get up and go
We travel less and we slow down a lot
But precious memories just seem to grow.

PERSEVERANCE

Perseverance requires the grit to keep on grinding
When the troubles pile up and our way is not clear
Digging down deeply when we feel we are beaten
Fighting tenaciously for our values in spite of our fear.

It's a challenge to stay optimistic when things are bleak
Maintaining an inner toughness when we want to quit
Resisting a life threatening illness that saps our strength
Defeating the demon of discouragement by breaking its grip.

Where does it come from this persistence to overcome
Taking one more step and not throwing in the towel
We need help and encouragement from family and friends
We pray to our Maker and sometimes we just howl.

We strengthen our bodies when we show persistent grit
We take comfort that our Lord walks with us all the way
Relying on Him completely as we struggle through our pain
Knowing through Him we can break through someday.

MEDICINES

We all develop aches, pains, illnesses and need surgery.
"Aging," as pundits have said, "is not for sissies"
God in his wisdom provided plants for healing
In modern times we distill ingredients we call medicine.

Even the young need medicines, it is a human condition
The pulsing pain cries out for relief so we take a pill
Grateful to those who use their skills to stimulate healing
Hoping that we can endure and live wholly once again.

The arsenal of modern medicines staggers the imagination
Costly elixirs holding promise for the desperate and despairing
Illnesses once considered fatal now within the bounds of hope
Medicines provide a comforting antidote to our human vulnerability.

Like all good things in life, medicines can turn harmful and betray
Pills taken too long can produce an addiction or result in our demise
We hold in our hands the keys to life and death if we use them wisely
Medicines can rule us or cure us, the choice is typically ours to make.

Medicines for some are an anathema used only as a last resort
Healthful living, sound diets, and regular exercise are recommended
Such practices have much to commend them and they are useful
I'm glad, though, that medicines stand ready to help when I am ailing.

PAIN

Pain is an unwanted friend
Warning us of lurking danger
Reminding us of our mortality
Telling us something is wrong.

Pain is an unremitting nuisance
Robbing us of our daily comfort
Troubling us with sharp unease
Piercing our serenity with a jolt.

Friend or foe pain is a regular presence
It lurks unseen but bursts into flames
We scream in agony as it tears at us
Searing, piercing pain can destroy.

Our mortal bodies must live a life of pain
It's the world we're destined to on this earth
Perhaps pain is why we long for heaven
When we say goodbye forever to this intrusion.

There are lessons of compassion to be learned
We need to help those trapped by unyielding pain
Humans all fall victim to this troubling vexation
Reminding us to forget self and comfort one another.

GUILT

Guilt is a subtle, unsettling conviction
Reminding us we have done wrong
It is one of God's purifying emotions
Stabbing our conscience like a prong.

Guilt helps us change and make amends
It is designed to guide us along life's path
"No one is perfect," is an oft repeated claim
Relying on this excuse is simply bad math.

Guilt is essential in this human domain
There is far too much evil on the loose
Without the nagging sense of guilt inside
The world would have even more abuse.

Like all things meant for our ultimate good
Guilt can paralyze us and do much harm
Folks can be falsely shamed into hurting silence
Sensing deep guilt when there is no such alarm.

God has provided a way to deal with our guilt
Be sorry, ask forgiveness, choose a different way
We all make mistakes and may repeat them again
God's infinite forgiveness takes guilt away.

CARING

Humans have a deep need to be nurtured
We are wrenched from the womb into a new land
However long we live thereafter we seek security
Perhaps it is a longing to return to our mother's hand.

Even in maturity, perhaps especially then, we crave caring
The culture, however, frequently demands a tougher mien
"Get over it," "suck it up," "stop the pity party," "grow up"
Such advice, though well meaning, hurts every human being.

The Holy Writ challenges us to love one another as ourselves
How does this translate into what we do with our daily lives?
For some it means having noble thoughts of what they might do
Others become real and help those who are suffering to survive.

We need nurturing, caring, a helping hand, a cheerful smile
We may hide this need with fake bravado and macho talk
The wise among us admit their need and humbly ask for help
The wiser still treat each human kindly aiding them in their walk.

OLD FRIENDS

Friendships are fragile in these internet days
Facebook friendships seem a poor substitute
We do see pictures and learn snippets of life
But achieving genuine friendship is probably moot.

We learn as we live that not much really counts
We get seduced by the things the ads all portray
We sadly learn that "things" don't bring happiness
It takes relationships with people to make our day.

Relationships are the key to living a vibrant life
Our relationship to our Maker should be in first place
The time spent with people to listen, help, and learn
Is the secret to satisfaction in this great human race.

In this fast-paced, throw things away quickly, modern world
Friendships can seem an anachronism, something lost in the past
Then we meet old friends again, some we have known from our youth
We learn anew this truth: Old friendships are precious; they last.

CHILLING

Even in maturity our lives can be frantic
Doctor's appointments, surgeries, pain
Falls, illnesses, kids still messing up
What can we do to stop all the strain?

Many books are out there to offer advice
Diet, exercise, yoga, prayer and meditation
An endless array of strategies to choose
We'd like to find a quick path to salvation.

Our times conspire in a fast, wired existence
We connect anywhere at the touch of a key
But electronic communication can leave us wanting
There is no substitute for the humbly bent knee.

We must center ourselves and connect with our maker
Breathe deeply in gratitude and try to be still
Our frantic pursuits can steal joy and happiness
Learn to slow down and by trusting just chill.

HOSPITALS

Our bodies are precious gifts from God
Marvelous structures that serve us faithfully
But in maturity time has flown and takes it toll
Falls, accidents, and illnesses can happen rapidly.

Grave illnesses can shock with their rapidity
Compelling us to reach a hospital "now"
The EMS workers rush to attend us
Illnesses can force all of us to bow.

Hospitals are crucial we can't do without them
But long corridors and hallways can be cold
The need for efficiency and sometimes urgent care
Can intimidate a patient and make them feel old.

There are papers to sign and tests to endure
The schedule seems arbitrary, strange noises abound
You are awakened at night to see if you are alive
Another blood test is taken as the nurse makes her round.

"The doctor will come soon," is a promise often made
But patience is essential if you expect one by noon
Food seems to appear just when visitors arrive
A nurse surfaces for more testing crowding the room.

In spite of the trials that a hospital stay entails
We thank God that such institutions can keep us alive
The doctors and nurses and aides have diligently served
We're grateful for our recovery and give them a "high five."

DOCTOR'S VISITS

We are blessed to be fully alive
To have a living, breathing body
Alas, in living long some aches emerge
That are not cured by a hot toddy.

So seniors often must schedule visits
For doctors and specialists and lots of tests
It's a frequent event on our weekly calendar
To help us get rid of our latest health pest.

We wonder why they can't schedule better
As we sit and wait and read old mags
"Our time is valuable too," we sputter
We mentally complain as the time drags.

Finally the nurse will call our name
We meekly smile and try to act nice
We're weighed and ushered in to wait
Doc keeping to schedule is simply "no dice."

The door opens and the doctor enters
We're relieved that now we'll get attention
He listens briefly as we report our symptoms
Our long wait, of course, gets no mention.

We look for clues in the doctor's demeanor
Does he think we're curable one more time
Or perhaps he's puzzled and needs more tests
To this we respond: "That will be fine."

We leave relieved but somewhat doubtful
The latest pain can make us mope
More pills, more tests, more interventions
We may be failing, but we have hope.

Doctor's visits are necessary in senior living
We share our stories of the latest test
We pray and ponder our many challenges
Thanking God, knowing we are blessed.

LEFT BEHIND

The breathe of life is a vital essence
Made poignant in a painful loss
When a loved one is taken from us
And the hurt pierces our very soul.

Time helps heal the experts say
The hurting grows less mercifully
The loss is embedded in visceral tracings
Never fully extinguished but subtly receding.

Perhaps this is God's profound plan
Honoring a time when two lives meshed
Gently affirming the spiritual connection
Of a love that in eternity will live forever.

For those left behind the sorrow is deep
One can smile and be brave but the hurt really aches
We need comforting friends and God's gentle touch
We can trust Him to heal us and guide every day.

Section 3

OLIOS

—ᴍ—

This section contains miscellany. The poems illustrate life issues, opinion, and the vagaries of human existence. Ponder them. May you be encouraged to rise above any biases, prejudices, or preconceptions and, with your actions, help bring sanity to a world that sometimes seems to be falling apart.

SUCCESS

Like a narcotic people crave success
In small things or large we get an infection
It is a good thing when held in proportion
It robs us when we obsess over perfection.

No one likes to fail so seeking success is sane
The problem comes when success dominates
Nothing short of success seems to satisfy
Falling short produces a series of berates.

Happiness requires perspective and gratefulness
Excessive pursuit of success fogs our happiness lens
We see others as more worthy while we are failures
We strive for unsatisfying prizes that rate "tens."

"Get a life," is advice often tossed about in jest
Sometimes the truth is hidden in such little vignettes.
Living is meant to be full of love, sharing, and joy
A self-centered success obsession brings ultimate regret.

THE NON-APOLOGY

You hear it constantly
Embarrassed public figures
Politicians exposed for malfeasance
Squirming out of responsibility.

"If I have offended anyone,"
The phony explanation begins
"Then I apologize,"
The subterfuge continues.

They do it with a straight face
Seemingly unmindful of their hubris
"Iffing" their way out of the wrong
A sincere apology contains no "if."

Spinelessly they cover their shame
So "if" no-one is offended, they retract it?
What if they simply admitted they were wrong?
Humbly asking for forgiveness?

A straightforward apology is simple
State the wrong and admit responsibility
Apologize for the wrong and ask forgiveness
The "if" apology is an abomination.

The mass media contribute complicity
Recording the wimpiness without confrontation
Our sense of propriety and decency are skewered
On "if I have offended anyone" non-apologies.

SPORTS

We Pinnacle people dearly love our sports
In earlier times we got out there and played
Now it's card games, chair exercises and such
We've "matured" and become far more staid.

But the passions still burn when we root for our team
Football, baseball, basketball, or the sport of the day
We faithfully follow their winning and their follies
We watch and fantasize and wish we could still play.

The San Antonio Spurs are a team most of us cheer
They're the "good guys" who modestly still win a lot
With teamwork and sharing they somehow prevail
But in close games our stomachs get tied in a knot.

In college football our choices run across the land
Our loyalties have faded but we still love our school
We are Aggies, and Longhorns, and Okkies and more
If you don't root for our team we think you're a fool.

We fuss about high salaries and the false pride displayed
Modern athletes are worshiped and coddled like sin
We still hang in through trades, drugs, and anomalies
Sports grip our psyches when we lose or hopefully win.

INCOME TAX

We know that taxes are the price of liberty
The government really does need our money
But the wars, waste, and foolish regulations
Create deep resentments that are not funny.

The income tax is supposed to be fair
You are taxed upon the money you earn
But loopholes exist for many exemptions
And government seems to have money to burn.

The corporations and wealthy seem to prosper
No matter the tax rate or the forms to be filed
The average citizen is hopelessly outclassed
No wonder the IRS is resisted and reviled.

The politicians continually claim they'll do right
If we just elect this one we'll have a fair deal
Post election, however, the average guy is forgotten
Don't complain, pay your taxes, or the heat you will feel.

MODERN MEDIA

Modern media marvels stagger the imagination
Devices held in our hand powerfully inform
Instantly bringing news from distant places
No crisis too small, a report on each storm.

The benefits of such abundance are transforming
We could be the most informed generation of all
Yet, we pay a steep price for this hyper society
Former standards of validity have taken a fall.

Our newspapers have suffered trying to compete
Genuine reporters who used to hold feet to the fire
Have been downsized and silenced by conflicting voices
Replaced by ill informed bloggers who covet and conspire.

The cable channels now offered in great profusion
Air biases with conviction that they have the news right
Too many Americans rely on such single flawed sources
The regular news channels have lost their esteemed might.

Democracy requires diligence by citizens who discern truth
We can lose this great nation by corruption from within
Politicians pander freely in this modern media confusion
We must wake up and think clearly or our country won't win.

SMART PHONES

Who coined this term for a modern ubiquity
Phones that do more than we understand
Instruments that some can not lay aside
Walking or driving with one in their hand.

The latest contraptions are marvels for sure
Challenging our brains and our dexterity
Why should a "smart phone" make us feel so dumb
When we timorously respond with uncertain perplexity.

We'd be happy just to make a convenient phone call
Modern phones are too smart to leave it that way
We get email and messages and answers prolifically
We get flustered and flummoxed and call it a day.

Our kids are in sync with smart phone idiosyncrasies
For them our mysteries and hangups seem obscure
I'm afraid that the "smarts" of modern technology
Is a continuing development we'll just have to endure.

PHOTOGRAPHS

What causes humans to seek immortality
Posing with family and friends at odd places
Smiling awkwardly trying to act happy
Saving the images for later embraces.

In older days a photo was a bit more rare
Film was expensive and quickly ran out
Now our smart phones mindlessly click
Ubiquitous memories we show off and tout.

A photograph album was once like fine art
Carefully arranged with captions on top
Now there is no room to store such artifacts
So we quietly dispose not telling mom or pop.

There is an allure when we see old photographs
Laughing at the styles noting most folks were thin
But who are these people staring back from the past
We can't always remember but we smile at their grin.

Photographs will remain a vital part of our life
Technology may cheapen images but cannot erase
The human desire to capture people, events and places
Memories are precious we must each claim our space.

DRESS

A person can be judged by what they wear
It's cruel but frequently true
People judge us by how we look
Rather than by what we are or do.

We know you can't judge a book by its cover
But with people it's not that easy
We admire folks that look classy in clothes
And look down on unkempt as quite queasy.

What lesson is learned from this human trait
For we typically want to appeal and to please
But obsessing over garments and needless glitter
Can bring us a life that's just a tease.

Be willing to confidently live life as you
Pleasing others is merely a trap
Wear something decent, of course
But you're worth far more than your wrap.

WRINKLES

I like wrinkles, they are not a sin
Not everyone will agree
Wrinkles reflect the test of time
They look quite nice on me.

My face is wrinkled from forehead to chin
They came without my trying
I've learned to love my carved up face
It did no good to keep sighing.

My granddaughter made my eyes twinkle
"Smile, Nana," she thoughtfully commanded
I smiled broadly as she had requested
"No Nana, they're wrinkles," she cried

Now I realize that denial no longer suffices
Creams don't work, nor does ice
I simply face the fact that my face is just right
Thinking wrinkles disappear when I sleep at night.

TAXES

Who likes to pay taxes? Hardly anyone I know
They'll take all our money leaving nothing to show
This thought is an exaggeration sharply focused on fear
Still it seems strange that our taxes go up year after year.

Our government grows relentlessly needing more money
Bureaucracy expands and proliferates like a bunny
The salaries and perks rise for the politicians in power
While poor average Joe and Jane are hosed like a shower.

While this scenario that has been painted is partially true
It can not be said that all government we must eschew
Government is essential for daily living and our defense
But government spending more wisely is only common sense.

How more justice and efficiency can be brought to bear
Requires a diligent citizenry that is more fully aware
Citizens are responsible they must reassert their rule
So get involved, vote sensibly, or be taken for a fool.

VOTING

We understand that we should vote
It's a message we've often heard before
Yet, some people clearly close their minds
And ignorantly choose to simply ignore.

Our country was built on sacrifice
Historically life was tenuous and tough
Voting for leaders was a precious won right
With kings and queens we'd had enough.

The modern choices we have are sometimes lame
The vote is not always between good and the bad
Candidates waffle, shamelessly pandering to their base
After we vote we can sense that we've been had.

Voting requires a sharp focus to make an intelligent choice
Citizens must resist remaining in a careless party groove
Political Parties covet power and can lose sight of country
The pandering politicians we should finally remove.

Democratic government is always under threat
Diligence is required inconvenient as that may be
Be wise, sort through pleasing rhetoric with discernment
Only engaged citizens can maintain the right to be free.

COMPROMISE

I believe in my bones that I'm in the right
There is no reason for discussion or debate
Others might disagree but they are plain wrong
I'll stick to my guns and trust to my fate.

This attitude of certitude infects all of life
It's the root of many of our problems today
It tears up relationships and terminates peace
"No compromise" is simply arrogance on display.

In politics there is always a difference of thought
Judicious compromise has been a necessary tool
Where folks come together and get the job done
Today's fear of compromise makes Congress a fool.

Compromise is conceding that others have a point
Resisting every compromise is like holding on to hate
A mind that cannot change is always doomed to lose
Compromises with graciousness never go out of date.

POLITICS

We are taught in school we are a unique democracy
We have a precious right to steer our national boat
Enlightened leaders are vital to continue our freedom
Our self governance relies on whether we all vote.

As we mature we realize life is not that simple
Political parties form and direct the choices
Politicians gerrymander to provide safe districts
Money dominates and drowns out other voices.

Politicians become an entitled, privileged class
Elections still matter but far less than the past.
Loyalty to political party replaces love for our Nation
Normally sensible people accept lies that are vast.

Stalemate in government becomes the new normal
Vitriolic rhetoric replaces compromise, now deemed a sin
The Congress is deviously controlled by their money masters
That threaten to punish members if they ever give in.

Why didn't they teach these truths when we were in school
Warning against a political class that could make us a fool
We still have a vote but the people must wake up in alarm
Not a foreign land but our government is doing us harm.

We have a country deemed the envy of this entire Earth
Our military has sacrificed for our freedom and worth
Let us summon courage to fight like our patriotic pioneers
Replacing entrenched politicians to resounding cheers.

MIASMA

God has given us the power of language
Words to speak to change the world
Animals communicate beyond our ken
But they do not have the power of words.

Humans alone have the uniqueness
To speak, to challenge, to destroy
The choice is ours to use this fire
To warm and comfort or be cruel.

Words themselves can be tricky
They carry meaning through context
They may seem beautiful but contain poison
They must be chosen with loving care.

I looked intently at the word "miasma"
"Pretty," I thought, attracted by the spelling
"Mi" for me, the "a," sound of the universe
"Ma" a familial sound for a precious mother.

Unpacked, the word delighted me
Alas, learning the meaning changed the flow
"Unwholesome vapor as rising from marshes
Befogging the atmosphere."

Surprised, I was reminded of the obligation
We hold through the great power of the tongue
What would happen to this seething planet
So plagued by violence and selfish mien.

If each human voice would cloak itself in love
Seeking words that truly inspire and support
Rejecting miasmic, poisoned, vaporous speech
Reclaiming language for healing our world.

HEROES

Who are the heroes in this stricken age?
Someone to admire for a great deed done
Sports figures and actors display their talents
Their fame is vaporous and soon un-won.

We turn to our military for acts of valor
Soldiers risking all for comrades in arms
Generals, even grunts seem far more worthy
Than athletes and those who rely on charm.

However it is difficult not to be disillusioned
All our heroes are clad in flesh and blood
They glitter in public for a brief moment
Rumor and envy can pull them down in the mud.

When we think more deeply than look for fame
We understand being "heroic" calls for denying oneself
Then our thoughts respond to the great ones around us
Moms, dads, strangers, and old folks who get off the shelf.

Heroes are all around us if we simply open our eyes
Folks dying bravely, sharing generously, acting sacrificially
Neighbors who with acts of kindness teach us a truth
We all have it within us to be heroic and heed someone's plea.

CHRISTMAS GOOSE
INTRODUCTION

The "Christmas Goose" was intended to be a children's book
replete with colorful pictures to stimulate the child's imagination.
Alas, the artist never arrived. But we do have the words.

Jesus once said: "Unless you become as a little child you will not
enter the Kingdom of Heaven." He also said: "The Kingdom
is within you." This wisdom tell us unless we open our eyes
to the world as a little child we will miss much of its wonder.

As mature adults we can let our spiritual vision ossify.
We can close ourselves out of the marvels of life.
Let this poem help. Pretend you are reading it to a child,
perhaps your grandchild or great grandchild, or actually do it.
Let the whimsy amuse you. Be a child again.

THE CHRISTMAS GOOSE

By John Ellis

**The Christmas Goose
Had his neck in a noose
So he said to his friends gathered round.**

**I'd like to get loose
From this terrible noose
And go meet my friends in the town.**

**So they pulled on the noose
And he finally got loose
And he waddled off without a sound.**

**When he reached the town square
Crowds of people were there
Who looked at him with a big frown.**

**They wanted to nab him
And poke him and grab him
To cook til he reached golden brown.**

**But he dove under a stall
And escaped from them all
And scurried from that terrible town.**

**He returned to the farm
His luck changed like a charm
He was not needed for dinner at all.**

So he lived out his days
Through the rain and sun's rays
Enjoying summer, winter, spring and the fall.

Life is quite good for this goose
Who got loose from the noose
Who now says: "I'm really having a ball."

Section 4

SPIRITUAL

—ɯ—

Humans are in essence spiritual beings. Regardless of denomination, belief, or non-belief, we each sense deep down that we are drawn to a Creator. This section expresses the poet's conception of how God is reflected in our lives, and how gratefulness and compassion can help create a more loving world.

JESUS

" Who do you say I am?" Jesus asked
That's a question we all must answer
It's a profound issue provoking differences
Regrettably, religions take opposite views.

For Muslims Jesus is a holy man, a prophet
But he is not God nor the unique Son of God
Some religions say he is a good, righteous man
But they, too, deny that he is God.

Even within Christianity divisions arise
Degrees of divinity or humanity divide us
Sects form, churches split, rancor emerges
"Who do you say I am?" remains for all.

I believe he is God, sent by God to save us
He died on a cross to provide salvation for us
He rose from the grave to show victory over death
He set an example of how to live and He awaits us.

The concepts are at once simple and deeply complex
A humble believer can know truth and scholars ponder
Not all the questions can be answered on this earth
The central one of "who is He" is knowable to everyone.

Believe in Him, Trust Him, and follow Him is the answer
Differences in style and forms of worship don't matter
Jesus loves us and doesn't care about minor matters
By loving Him and loving others you live victoriously.

OXYGEN

We mortals need to breathe to live
Drawing oxygen from the atmosphere
That colorless, tasteless, gaseous blessing
God's gift to sustain us while we are here.

Oxygen is essential for life even for combustion
It is the most common element in the earth's crust
Lighting fire for our use and its essence for existence
Oxygen becomes for each of us an absolute must.

In maturity sometimes our lungs begin to fail
Those precious organs that take in life's breath
We supplement nature with machines and bottles
Tethered to our nostrils to give our breath depth.

Do our souls need oxygen, too, to reflect God's love
Is this how God replenishes his connection to Him
We are called to love Him and share his love with all
His precious oxygen vitalizes and deeply cleanses within.

KENYA CALLING

Kenya is a tantalizing, promising nation
It's a far, far away African land
Tribal rivalry and poverty abound
Needing provision from God's loving hand.

Warring factions and economic plight
Kenya is stymied by work that's undone
Too little education, corruption corroding
They need to hear that Christ has come.

Who will dare carry this message abroad?
Christ died for our sins; he is willing to save
He took our sins on himself; he went to the cross
He arose from the dead to conquer sin and the grave

He asks for belief in Him; simple trust
It's not your good works that will give you a lift
It's belief in Christ as your Savior and Lord
That brings eternal life--God's incredible gift.

Christ urged us to harvest; noting workers were too few
Will you obey and respond to his Great Commission?
The Spirit is moving; there are people in great need
The world is calling; will you respond to His mission?

PRAISE

Everyone likes validation and encouragement
We can all get tired and battered down
Life is filled with treacherous encounters
Sometimes we feel that we will drown.

Praise is a lubricant that lifts the soul
It is a miracle substance available to all
Rescuing us from bleak discouragement
It's a spiritual pick-up after we fall.

What prevents us from using this precious gift
To help heal the hurts and restore another's elan
Are we too self-centered, jealous, or neglectful
To love one another and follow God's plan.

There is much to commend when we open our eyes
We can see simple deeds and and heroic ones too
Being authentic with our praise is also required
Genuine compliments and praise everyone can do.

When we focus on praise instead of what's wrong
It changes the climate wherever we might go
Praise for our Maker keeps the praise force flowing
Praise in its essence rids the world of its woe.

FEARING

"Fear not," the Bible tells us
We hear the warning but our flesh fails
Fear infects our thinking and shrinks us
We don't do what we could but turn tail.

Why do we let fear paralyze us into inaction
Some fears are valid and we are wise to stop
More frequently we worry how we will appear
We fear failure or ridicule and our hopes pop.

We see "cool" folks among us act with elan
"I'd like to be like them," we often fantasize
The daring we resolve to demonstrate evaporates
We cravenly withdraw as if hiding our eyes.

Sometimes our fears impact our elections
We choose men and women we do not like
The sanity and morality that should govern us
Gets replaced by fear; we don't do what's right.

We can learn to make fear a friend not a foe
It begins by remembering we are created by God
He wants us to honor Him by living a life of love
So trust Him; follow the footsteps that Jesus has trod.

BUZZARDS

I see them from my Pinnacle window
Majestically spreading their wings to soar
Exuberantly catching the currents they glide
Diving and turning, buzzards at their core.

On the ground they are awkward, somewhat ugly
Created by the Great Designer to clean the land
Heads without feathers so they can do dirty work
Creatures who gather to dry and rest with their clan.

What can we learn from one of God's creations?
Much if we meditate and inform our mind
We sometimes live life awkwardly and stumble
Falling short in our actions time after time.

We are not bound by our many failures
God forgives and inspires us far more
When we love Him and help one another
On spiritual wings, like buzzards, we soar.

THE CHAPEL

Beautiful, stained glass windows surround
Biblical tales portrayed in colorful symbols
Telling us this is a special space, even holy
A Chapel, some might call "God's house."

Faith based beginnings called for a Chapel
Spirit led elders wanted space to worship
The Chapel erected to reverently serve people
A site dedicated to God years before the Pinnacle.

Now new buildings grace the Eden Hill community
The Chapel still calls out to come and worship
Gracefully the Chapel serves as activity space
Sacred or secular the Chapel welcomes all.

Its special place centers on its holy beauty
Funerals are held and provide comforting peace
Weddings, dinners, musicals, exercise, all enjoy
The timeless beauty of space dedicated to God.

No temple or man-made edifice can contain God
Yet structures built to honor him have a special spirit
Gathering to worship Him and pray and sing praises
Elevates the soul and takes us to our spiritual home.

WORSHIP

How can we reach a deep sense of awe
Our mind totally focused on the sublime
When our spirit seems to touch the master
And we are carried beyond the me and mine.

There lies within each of us a source of wonder
We can connect and know there is a higher power
When our mind spiritually kneels in reverence
And love, joy, and gratefulness begin to flower.

Life has its way of intruding and diverting us
We pursue careers, family, money, and health
Fret and worry corrode our spiritual connection
We forget that God is the true fountain of wealth.

We don't have to be evil to lose sight of the good
Simply focusing on ourselves can take us off course
Reclaiming worship requires humility even remorse
Being thankful to God, honoring Him as the Source.

GO WHERE?

"Where should I go?" We earnestly ask
Understanding that Jesus said: "Go."
Where? Into all the world
Why? Telling people about Jesus, and Baptising
In the name of the Father, Son and Holy Spirit
Teaching them to obey Christ's commandments
And Jesus promised: "I will go with you."

We wonder, what does that mean for me?
Where should I go. We think. We pray.
To Africa or simply across the street?
Tell me, Lord, speak clearly so I understand
We're compelled to pray, read the Bible and pray again
Sometimes with no clear direction that emerges
Left to discern our Great Commission with confusion.

Does that mean going is not for me?
Did Christ omit me when commissioning the disciples?
Why then did Christ say the fields are white but workers few?
The scriptures are clear we are each commanded to go
Understanding the Great Commission is not just a destination
We all go, daily we go, perhaps unknowingly as living witnesses
Then, "go;" take God's agape love and share it: EVERYWHERE.

DANCE ON UP

"Times up," the Good Lord said
"Your race is almost run.
I've let you see the whole of life
The pain, the quest, the fun."

My choices now have narrowed
As I lie pondering with a moan.
I can pity myself, fill up with regrets
Or stand tall till I'm finally home.

I've chosen to stand, frail tho I am
And dance like a playful pup.
Sing one last song—pray one last prayer
And dance my way on up.

God has been good these many years
Though I've had my doubts—lacked trust.
He's carried me safely in good times and bad
He promised I would not go bust.

So "warts and all," I've hung in strong
Focused deep on His promises made.
Diligently running my race in the sun
Knowing He would supply needed shade.

I rise up, then, completely in trust
More bent over, more rocking than roll.
Mind clear, faith intact, proclaiming aloud
That God in Christ Jesus saves souls.

Goodbye, darling wife, dear family and friends
I love you, I'll leave you and wait.
Till you run your race and you get your call
God willing, I'll be right by the gate.

No man and no woman can fully know
What their span of years will be.
But a choice for Christ sincerely made
Is the choice with a real guarantee.

Thank you, Lord, for my life, every breath
For forgiveness, for joys, even pain.
I've had fun, kept on chugging and growing
And danced whether sunshine or rain.

Life's over now—yes, too quickly it sped
Just a vapor, the race I have run
I go with joy in my heart, smile on my face
And the hope He tells me: "Well done."

Made in the USA
Middletown, DE
20 February 2022

61579723R00051